MW00451948

This journal belongs to

Stylized
WORKBOOKS

Stylized
WORKBOOKS

For permission requests contact: info@stylizedworkbooks.com

Check out our catalog at

STYLIZEDWORKBOOKS.COM

Made in United States
North Haven, CT
16 September 2023

41606237R00068